ultra sports

ultra marathon running

ultra marathon running

by Chris Hayhurst

the rosen publishing group's
rosen
central

Published in 2002 by The Rosen Publishing Group, Inc.
29 East 21st Street, New York, NY 10010

Copyright © 2002 by The Rosen Publishing Group, Inc.

First Edition

Library of Congress Cataloging-in-Publication Data

Hayhurst, Chris.
Ultra marathon running / by Chris Hayhurst.— 1st ed.
p. cm. — (Ultra sports)
Including bibliographical references (p.) and index.
Summary: Examines the world of exceptionally long running races and the athletes who run them.
ISBN 0-8239-3557-4 (lib. bdg.)
1. Marathon running—Juvenile literature. 2. Marathon running—History—Juvenile literature. 3. Runners (Sports)—Biography—Juvenile literature. [1. Marathon running. 2. Running. 3. Runners (Sports)] I. Title. II. Series.
GV1065 .H33 2002
796.43'52—dc21

2001003841

Manufactured in the United States of America

Contents

As you read this, something big is taking place. It's happening through-out the world, in places as different as the outback of Australia, the Himalayas of Nepal, and the South Pole. It's happening in oceans, lakes, and rivers. It's happening in the mountains, the desert, and the plains. It's probably even happening in your own backyard.

What is it? Well, if you've ever pushed yourself to the limit—gone faster, farther, longer, or harder than you ever thought possible—you know exactly what it is. It has nothing to do with money. It has nothing to do with fame. It's all about breaking boundaries—going that extra mile, so to speak. In modern-day lingo, it's all about "ultra."

Athlete running in the Himalayan Marathon

"Ultra" is extreme. It's beyond the normal, beyond what is expected. Ultra sports are athletic events that take things up a notch. They take what is ordinary—say, a 10-mile run—and make it extremely unordinary, adding to the run a 30-mile bike ride, 6 miles of cross-country skiing, and 4 miles of snowshoeing, all at an elevation of 10,000 feet. They turn a simple mountain bike race into a twenty-four-hour test of endurance to see who can ride the farthest. They double or quadruple the standard marathon so that runners must cover 50, 75, or even 100 miles of terrain. Events can last for hours, days, or weeks. Athletes spend months training for competitions—usually not because they hope to win, but because they just want to finish.

Ultra sports are becoming more and more popular every day. Often, participants are solo athletes, drawn to the challenge of going one-on-one with their own bodies and minds. Others take a different approach, preferring to race in organized competitions or as part of a team. Whatever the case may be, accomplished ultra athletes all have one thing in common: drive. They're driven to succeed. They set goals and achieve them, and they never say "I can't." They know how to win—if not the race, then the battle of mind over matter. Ultra athletes do not give up. They run, walk, bike, hike, swim, paddle, climb, and do whatever it takes to finish. And then, when they're done (and after a decent rest), they get right back up and do it again.

The date was June 18, 2000. It was a beautiful Sunday morning in Queens, New York, with somewhat cloudy skies and temperatures in the mid-70s. By all accounts, it was a perfect day for a run. It was a perfect day to kick off the fourth annual Sri Chinmoy 3,100 mile race.

Four very talented athletes, three men and one woman, toed the starting line. All four were experienced ultra runners. The woman, Suprabha Beckjord, had finished the race in each of the three previous years. The previous year's runner-up was there. The competition would be stiff. At 6:08 AM, following a short, silent meditation, the race began.

The Sri Chinmoy is no ordinary footrace. In fact, it's the longest certified race in the world. And to make it even more interesting, it takes place on one half-mile

A runner holds a flaming peace torch as she runs the Sri Chinmoy on March 6, 1997.

loop of concrete. The runners, all of whom are experienced at running very long distances, must cope not only with the tremendous physical stress of covering an average of 60 miles every day for almost two months but also with the mental challenge of repeating the same circle more than 5,600 times. It's not exactly a walk in the park. Races like this cannot be described in mere words. You have to watch the competitors as they trot by, read the expressions on their faces, and see the muscles in their legs and arms. The winner of the Sri Chinmoy 2000, twenty-nine-year-old Pekka Aalto from Helsinki, Finland, ran 70 miles on that first day. During his last week, days 43 through 48, he ran 68 miles, 66 miles, 67 miles, 66 miles, and 66 miles. On the final day, August 4, 2000, he ran 53 miles. His official time: 47 days, 13 hours, 29 minutes, 55 seconds.

Welcome to the world of ultra marathon racing. An ultra marathon is a running race that is longer than an official marathon. Technically speaking, a marathon is any running race over 26 miles, 385 yards (42.2 kilometers, 195 meters). Ultra runners, as they're known, run ultra marathons on all kinds of surfaces in all kinds of places. They run on paved roads in huge cities, on dirt trails in remote mountain ranges, and even on 400-meter tracks on high-school athletic fields. Ultra marathons are hard. Don't let any ultra runner tell you otherwise.

Deep Roots

Ultra marathons have been around for a very long time. Back in the 1800s, ultra marathoning was known as pedestrianism. A pedestrian is a person who gets around on foot. Typical pedestrianism events lasted for six days, and competitors would see how far they could travel on foot in that time.

Before pedestrianism—for that matter, throughout history—ultra running took another form: message delivery. Runners covered extreme distances not for the athletic challenge but to carry important messages from one place to another. That was before the postal service, of course.

Today ultra marathon running is a far cry from what it used to be. It's now an official international sport recognized by the International Amateur Athletic Federation, the athletics governing body that oversees sporting events throughout the world.

Today there are two main types of ultra marathons. The first type is one in which runners must cover a specific distance. The distance depends on where the race is run, but typical events clock in at anywhere from 30 to 100 miles. Sometimes runners race from one town to another many miles away. Or they run to a turnaround point and then return to the start. On tracks or other measured short courses, runners go around and around in loops until they cover the required distance.

The other standard ultra running event requires runners to cover as many miles as possible within a set period of time. For example, twenty-four-hour races often take place on tracks. Runners circle the track for twenty-four hours straight. In the end, the person who goes the farthest wins.

Some ultra marathon races are held on fixed tracks.

Some ultra marathons are extremely long. The Trans America Footrace, for example, is almost 3,000 miles long. Each year racers in this event run and walk every day for almost two months to cover the entire distance from Los Angeles to New York.

Official Ultra Marathon World Records

50 km—2:43:38 (Thompson Magawana)
100 km—6:16:41 (Jean-Paul Praet)
200 km—15:57:50 (Yiannis Kouros)
30 mile—2:37:31 (Thompson Magawana)
40 mile—3:45:39 (Andy Jones)
50 mile—4:50:51 (Bruce Fordyce)
100 mile—12:05:43 (Andy Jones)
1,000 mile—12 days, 20 hours, 14 minutes, 27 seconds (Georgs Jermolajevs)
12 hour—159,750 meters (Andy Jones)
24 hour—290,221 meters (Yiannis Kouros)
48 hour—408,773 meters (Yiannis Kouros)
6 day—1,028,370 meters (Yiannis Kouros)

Because races are so long, and runners exert so much energy just to finish, competitors eat and drink along the way. They also sleep if the race is longer than a couple of days. In addition, most ultra runners don't run the entire length of any race. Usually they

A couple of weeks ago I ran a 100-kilometer fund-raiser for a child who is suffering from cancer. The bills are getting to be too much for her family. We raised about $2,000 and had a great time in the process!

—Ultra runner, Canada

walk on uphill sections and run on the flats and the downhills. If they were to try to run the entire race, they would eventually become too tired to keep going. Their legs would just give up.

If you think you have the legs to be an ultra runner, read on. Just don't forget to lace up first!

Becoming a runner is easy. Just throw on a pair of shorts and a T-shirt, lace up your running shoes, and hit the pavement. Getting started in ultra running, on the other hand, takes work. You see, unless you're an incredibly gifted athlete, you can't just jump headfirst into the ultra running scene. You have to work your way up and train your body and your mind for long distances. Only when you're physically able to handle 30, 50, or 100 miles of running should you ever attempt to run such a distance. In fact, the majority of organized ultra marathon events don't allow kids to race. They don't want inexperienced or poorly trained runners, who might end up injured, on the course.

Learning to Run

So first things first! Learn to run! One great way to learn to run is by playing

Take advantage of the supervised training that high-school athletic programs offer.

sports at school. Soccer and field-hockey players can run several miles in one game. Or join your school track or cross-country teams. Track events usually involve runs of two miles or less, while cross-country events can be much longer.

The advantage of joining a team is that you'll learn to run and will get in shape under the watchful eye of a coach. Coaches can teach you how to stretch, show you ways to increase your speed and endurance, and keep you motivated. Plus, it's fun to train and compete as part of a team!

If the thought of joining a team doesn't sound appealing, all is not lost. Running comes naturally to many people. Go ahead and give it a try on your own at a local track or a footpath. Just be sure to start slowly. Remember, as a beginning ultra runner, you need endurance. You can build up speed later, when your body is ready.

Another way to get involved in the running scene is by joining your local running club. Many small towns and most cities have organized groups that get together on a regular basis to go running. They run in new places all the time to keep things interesting and sometimes even supplement the runs with special track workouts designed to improve technique, strength, and speed. Ask people at your local running store if they know of any running clubs in the area.

Finally, see if local youth groups and organizations offer running clinics or stage special running events for kids. You might find a whole community of young runners just like yourself. And, if you're lucky, you just might make some really good friends.

Oh, and one last thing. If you ever find yourself wondering just what the ultra running scene is really like, go to a race. Call the race director a month or two ahead of time and offer to volunteer on race day. He or she will probably be glad to have you help out, and you'll get to see all the action up close. Now that's the way to learn!

Becoming an Ultra Marathon Runner

Once you've learned to run, it's time to start thinking big—really big. The key to becoming a successful ultra marathon runner is mileage. Logging a lot of miles builds endurance. You have to train your body to run very long distances at a slow, steady pace.

The way to do this is simple: practice. Many ultra runners will make a long run a weekly part of the training routine. They'll run medium distances—like 6 to 10 miles—Monday through Thursday, do an easy run on Friday, then put in a very long run on Saturday. A typical Saturday run might range anywhere from 12 to 30 miles or more. Then, on Sunday, they'll take the entire day off. Sound like madness? It is, if you're not an ultra runner.

If you are an ultra runner, though, it's fun. To an ultra runner, it's the running itself—not just the finish—that's the draw.

Trail Running 101

When you run for long distances, sometimes the roads all start to look the same. For a change of pace, so to speak, many ultra runners turn to trail running.

Running on trails is quite different from running on roads. As the terrain is uneven, every step feels different than the last. One second you're on a flat dirt trail, the next you're high stepping over rocks and logs or sloshing through mud. Trails can be difficult to follow, even confusing. Often there are no signs to point you in the right direction, and there is no one else around to tell you where to go. You have to be handy with a map and compass, or if you're not, you should at least be familiar with the area in which you're running.

Most road runners find trail running to be incredibly challenging, even humbling, the first few times they go. It's almost impossible to run as fast on trails as you can on the road, mainly because the rough terrain requires lots of fancy footwork and balance. Also, steep hills, curvy switchbacks, and river and stream crossings

Runners have to mind their steps when trail running because the terrain is uneven and the course is often confusing.

inevitably reduce the pace, sometimes even forcing the best runners to walk.

Ultra runners have been known to go on four- or five-hour trail runs just for training. They drive or jog to the trailhead, stuff a fanny pack full of extra clothing, energy bars, and water bottles, and head for the hills. They eat and drink as they run and put on or shed layers of clothing as the weather permits. If you ever decide to go trail running, here are some things to keep in mind.

Clothing

Wear trail-running shoes. They're designed for the specific conditions you'll see on the trail and come in handy when the going gets rough.

Always dress in or carry running clothes that protect you from changing weather conditions. Even if it looks nice out, if you're going on a long run way out in the mountains, the weather can change fast. It pays to be prepared.

Your First Run

Start with an easy run on a flat trail. That way you'll get an idea of what it's all about before you have to tackle the big hills and tricky terrain.

Plan ahead. If the trail is an "out-and-back," make sure you turn around early enough so you can make it all the way back to the trailhead.

Be on the lookout for roots, rocks, and other obstacles, especially when you're tired.

Warm up before you begin. Stretch your legs and arms and walk for the first few minutes.

Keep your head up and your eyes on the trail ahead. Watch out for obstacles. Rocks, roots, logs, and branches can all send you sprawling.

Other Considerations

Stay on the trail, even when it's muddy or wet. When you cut switchbacks or go around difficult sections, you wind up killing plants and destroying the land near the trail.

Pace yourself. Trail running can be extremely tiring!

There's nothing better than spending hours alone or with friends on the road or the trail. So go on! What are you waiting for? Start running!

There's no doubt about it: When you're properly prepared and well conditioned, ultra running is downright fun. In races, competitors often help each other out, cheer each other on, and, after the finish, celebrate together. Runners call this camaraderie.

But ultra running, like any ultra-endurance sport, does have its downsides. And if you're not prepared, it can even be dangerous. If there's one thing you should think about when you start ultra running or training to become an ultra runner, it's your personal safety. Make safety your top priority and you're guaranteed to have a good time.

On the Road

Running on roads can be very dangerous. In fact, the car can be the pedestrian's worst enemy. Here's what to do when you go for a road run:

Stay visible. Wear brightly colored clothing so drivers can see you. If you run at night, in bad weather, or at dusk or dawn, wear a reflective vest or other reflective clothing. Also, always run against traffic, that is, on the left-hand side of the road.

Stop at intersections and make eye contact with drivers before you cross streets.

Run on sidewalks and bicycle and walking paths whenever possible. Otherwise, stay inside the white line, out of the driving lane.

Pick your routes carefully. Try to avoid narrow streets and roads with a lot of traffic.

On the Trail

Trail running—especially long-distance trail running—can also be dangerous. But unlike road running, cars are not the problem.

Plan ahead and be prepared for anything. Carry extra food and water. Carry clothing for all potential weather conditions.

Tell your friends or family where you're going before you leave. That way, if you get lost or hurt, they'll know where to look for you.

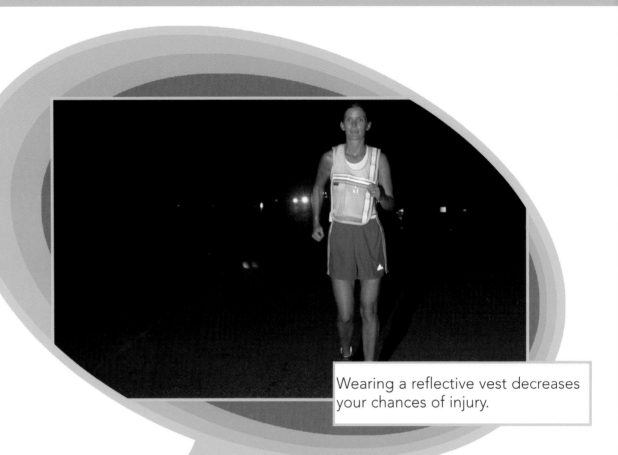

Wearing a reflective vest decreases your chances of injury.

Get the scoop on a new trail before you begin your run. You can do this by talking to the employees at a local sports store or by checking a guidebook.

Call the appropriate land-management agency—city, county, state, or federal, depending on where you're going—before you go, to ensure the trail is still safe and open to the public.

Avoid running trails that are too difficult for your level of fitness. Start with the easy trails, then work your way up to the harder ones.

If possible, run on well-traveled and well-marked trails.

Run with a partner.

Watch for rocks, roots, ice, and other hazards on the trail. If the trail becomes too dangerous, walk until you're in the clear.

At the Races

When you start running organized ultra marathons, you'll find that the level of race support varies from race to race. At some events, there will be absolutely no support at all. At these races, runners are entirely on their own from start to finish—unless they're lucky enough to have friends that can help them out. They have to fill their own water bottles from streams, carry their own food, and tend to any on-the-course injuries by themselves.

At major races with a lot of participants, aid stations are often available every five or ten miles. The stations usually consist of just a table or two set up alongside the course, or sometimes walk-in tents. They are staffed by race organizers or volunteers. They often include food, water, energy drinks, and emergency supplies, as

Volunteers fill cups with water to give to the runners.

well as trained emergency medical technicians ready to help runners who are seriously ill or hurt. Whether you enter a big race with a lot of support or a small race with little or no help from organizers, you should always arrive well prepared.

Preventing Injury

The best way to avoid getting hurt during ultra marathon running is by listening to your body. Your body will let you know when you need a rest. When it does, take its advice and take some time off.

Another key to keeping healthy is doing warm-ups before and cooldowns after every run. Warming up involves stretching your legs, arms, shoulders, neck, and back. It also means starting out slowly and easing into your running rhythm. Eventually, once you're feeling loose, you can pick up the pace a little. Cooling down is just like warming up. Slow your pace or even walk near the end of your run. Then, when you're done, spend time stretching all of your muscles.

Eating Right

Running is hard work—not only for your legs and feet but also for your entire body. To survive a long run, and to keep your body from breaking down, you need to eat right. Otherwise you won't have the energy to finish.

Think of your pre-run meal as a chance to put gas in your tank. If you're planning to go on a run in the early morning, eat a high-carbohydrate meal (like pasta, bread, and salad) for dinner the night before. Then, right before you go, eat a light snack—a banana seems to work for many runners. Whatever you do, try to avoid candy and other sweets. It might give you a quick boost at the start, but that energy won't last for long.

Experiment to see what you can handle and what works best for you. Some people can eat a peanut butter sandwich fifteen minutes before they run. Others must wait for hours after eating anything just so the food can be digested. Everyone is different.

If you're going on a long-distance run, you'll need to pack food for the trip. Most runners like to carry energy bars. They're lightweight and small enough to carry in a fanny pack, and there are many kinds that even taste good. Fruit is another good option for the long haul.

Snack as you go, before you lose your strength. If you eat a little bit of food every fifteen minutes or so, you should never run out of gas. Remember, food is fuel. So fill 'er up!

Drink Up!

It's very important to stay well hydrated when you run. Your body needs fluids to function, and the more you run, the more you sweat them out. Ultra runners

Be sure to drink a lot of fluids before, during, and after your long-distance run.

can lose gallons of water during a race. The only reason they don't collapse and die is because they know how to stay hydrated.

The key to staying hydrated, especially on a long run, is drinking every chance you get. Most long-distance runners carry a water bottle with them when they run, whether they carry it in their hand or attached to a fanny pack. That way they can take a sip every few minutes as they run and replenish fluids as soon as they are lost.

What you keep in your bottle is entirely up to you. Many runners drink plain old water. Others prefer special energy-boosting drinks designed to keep their bodies' electrolyte levels in balance. There are countless sports drinks on the market. Try a few out and see what works best for you.

It's a good idea to keep drinking water and other fluids before and after a long run, too. Drink up the day before your big run and during the hours immediately before you start. Make hydration a habit. Your body will thank you for it!

Running Gear

In case you're wondering, ultra running isn't football or hockey. You don't have countless pads to strap on and there's no need for cleats or skates. In fact, ultra running is what you might call a minimalist sport. You hardly need any gear to get started—just your legs, your lungs, and a good pair of running shoes.

Still, if you get serious and start to really rack up the miles, you'll probably need more gear. Ask almost any ultra runner what she relies on to get her to the finish line and she'll read you a list longer than the run itself. And, for every item she mentions, she'll tell you what's good and bad about a certain brand, where the best place is to get it, and how it has helped her in the past. Ultra athletes can be picky about what they will and will not carry on a run. What should you pack in your bag of tricks? Only you can decide.

Shoes

Unless you plan to run barefoot (not a good idea), you'll have to buy a good pair of running shoes. This means no cross-trainers or high-top basketball shoes or hiking boots. You'll need true running shoes. Running shoes are made specifically for running. If you run long distances in shoes not intended for running, you may wind up with serious foot, ankle, and knee problems. These injuries can quickly end a running career. At the shoe store, tell the salesperson you want running shoes. He or she will steer you in the right direction.

Running shoes are funny. They all look basically the same, and they're all pretty much designed for the same thing, yet ask any experienced runner if all shoes are alike and he or she will laugh in your face: "No way!"

You see, in reality, every shoe has its own unique personality. Some are narrow; some are wide. Some are made for women; some are for men. Some have big boxes for the toes; some have small ones. Some lace one way; others lace another way. Some are intended strictly for

Wearing a comfortable pair of good running shoes reduces the risk of developing an injury while running in an ultra marathon.

trails; others are only for paved roads. Still others are good for all kinds of terrain. Decide what your typical running surface will be. Then get shopping. You can plan on spending between $65 and $100 for your first pair of running shoes. That may sound like a lot of money, but considering it's the most important piece of equipment you'll need for your new sport, it's not a bad deal.

A good way to keep posted on the latest and greatest developments in running-shoe technology is by reading the shoe reviews in major running magazines. Most publications print a yearly list of their favorites. Just remember, the best pair of shoes for you may not be the best for the next person. Every shoe feels slightly different on every foot, so what might cause pain for a runner with flat feet might be perfect on a person with a big arch. Make the shoe's fit your number-one concern. Ask the salesperson to measure your feet, and be sure to wear your running socks when you try on shoes. Test many different brands and styles to find the best fit for you, then compare prices on the ones you like the most.

Buying Shoes: Trail or Road?

If you know you'll be running on trails instead of on roads, buy trail shoes. Trail shoes usually have a more aggressive, or rugged, tread than do road shoes. They are intended to help you manage tight turns and steep and slippery hills. The added support they provide may mean the difference between a speedy run and a sprained ankle. Otherwise, buy road shoes. They're usually a bit lighter than trail shoes are and may be more comfortable on long outings on the asphalt.

Finally, before you buy a pair of shoes, go for a test run. Many running stores set up treadmills for shoppers. Once you've laced up a pair of shoes, hop on the treadmill and run for a few minutes. That way you'll have an idea of how they'll feel out on the road.

Socks

It might sound silly, but when it comes to long-distance running, your socks can mean the difference between success and failure. With the wrong socks, or combination of socks, you can easily end up with painful blisters on your feet. And a blister, as you may already know, is the last thing you want when you're running.

Avoid blisters by wearing socks that fit comfortably inside your shoes.

It's an age-old question: Thick or thin? Some runners like thick socks. They say thick socks provide extra padding for the feet for every pounding step. Others swear by thins. These runners like the lightweight and increased sensitivity and the fact that their socks tend to dry out faster if they get wet.

Socks come in all kinds of materials. Cotton socks are comfortable when they're dry, but once they get wet, they stay wet. Socks made of polypropylene or other high-tech materials feel slick on your feet and are sometimes even waterproof. Many runners like to wear a thin pair of polypropylene socks as an underlayer and then double up with a second pair of thicker socks. Usually it depends on how their feet fit in their shoes. If your shoes are tight and formfitting, you probably need thin socks. If they are a bit roomy, you may need thick socks.

Summer Wear

The key to a good running shirt is comfort. You want to be comfortable no matter what the condition. If it's roasting out, you want to stay cool. If you are training in the mountains, you might encounter chilly conditions, even during summertime. If it's freezing, you need to keep warm. When it's wet, you've got to stay dry.

Tops

The best running shirts are made of lightweight polypropylene, capilene, silk, or other sweat-wicking, moisture-regulating fabrics. Thanks to their space-age designs, often the same style of shirt will keep you dry and warm in cool weather and cool and dry in the warm weather. Most come in long-sleeve or short-sleeve versions, so pick whatever works for your local climate. If there's rain in the forecast, you should carry a lightweight, waterproof rain jacket. And if it's windy, be sure to wear a windbreaker.

The risk of getting scorched makes a summer ultra marathon more challenging.

Bottoms

As a runner, you've got to take good care of your legs. In the summer this means wearing a pair of loose and lightweight running shorts. For cooler mornings you may need a pair of tights. And in the rain it helps to have waterproof protection, like a pair of rain pants.

Running shorts are usually made of nylon and come in lots of fun colors. They're as light as a feather and dry out in a matter of minutes. Go ahead and try a pair. Wear a pair just once and you'll never go back to your street shorts, at least not when you're running.

Other Warm-Weather Gear

When running in summer, your worst enemy may be the sun. Ultra runners spend a lot of time in the sun, and sunburns hurt. Wear sunscreen, a lightweight cap, sunglasses, a long-sleeve shirt, and any other protection you can think of to keep from getting scorched. Many runners carry cotton bandanas. White or light-colored bandanas can provide some shade for your head and neck in hot weather and can be drenched in water or wrapped around ice for instant cooling relief.

Winter Wear

Serious runners think nothing of hitting the roads and trails year-round, even in the dead of winter. But although running in winter is essentially the same thing as running during any other time of year, you have to know how to dress. Cold weather necessitates a few additional items of clothing, which you won't typically need in the summer sun.

Chafing

Chafing is one problem many ultra runners face. When wearing shorts, they often end up with chafed inner thighs. This happens when your thighs rub together over and over again until eventually they're rubbed raw. It can be very painful—enough to make you want to stop running altogether. A way to get around this problem is by wearing a pair of smooth bike shorts beneath your running shorts.

Tops

First off, forget about cotton. Leave it at home. Once cotton gets wet, it stays wet. If you're cold and wet at the same time, you can easily become hypothermic—a very serious health condition resulting from the loss of too much body heat.

Dress in layers. By wearing layers instead of just one bulky piece of clothing, you can shed clothes when you need to and keep your body temperature at just the right level. To do it right, you should have three layers: the base, the middle, and the outer.

The base layer is the shirt you wear directly over your skin. It should be made of polypropylene, capilene, or other high-tech moisture-controlling materials. This layer's main job is to keep your skin dry. The middle layer acts as an insulator from the cold yet allows moisture wicked by the base layer to easily pass through and escape. Lightweight fleece is a good middle layer.

Finally, the outer layer offers full protection from Mother Nature and all she throws at you. Waterproof shells seem to work best. Just be sure to wear one that is breathable—that is, it allows moisture to escape. Some tops have vents beneath the armpits and along the zippers or they may allow moisture to escape directly through the fabric itself.

Bottoms

When it's really cold, wear running tights. Running tights come in different thicknesses and fabrics designed for different temperatures. What you buy should depend on where you live and how cold your winters are. Polypropylene long underwear makes for a good base layer beneath tights on extremely cold days. If it's not downright freezing, just wear nylon or waterproof wind pants over a pair of shorts.

Other Cold-Weather Gear

Top off your winter wardrobe with a hat and gloves. You lose most of your body heat through your head, so a good hat is critical for staying comfortable during a long run. Wear a wool or polypropylene hat designed to wick sweat away yet insulate your ears and head from the cold. Gloves are important for keeping your hands warm. Again, avoid cotton gloves. If they get wet, your hands will be cold. Many runners wear thin fleece gloves beneath waterproof shells.

And Last but Not Least . . .

For everything you need to bring but don't want to wear or hold at the start of your run, wear a fanny pack. Fanny packs strap around your waist. You can stuff them with things like food, water, first-aid supplies, and extra clothing.

Many long-distance runners carry bottles filled with water or

It's important to wear layers if you are running in cold weather.

sports drinks. This is an especially good idea when you're running alone during training and there are no aid stations where you can stop to drink. You can hold the bottle in one hand or attach it to your fanny pack.

Finally, if you think you'll want to run at night or early in the morning when the sun isn't quite up, be sure to wear reflective clothing so that drivers can see you. An easy way to make regular running clothes reflective is by sewing or sticking on strips of reflective tape.

If there's one thing that's true about ultra running, it's that no race is easy. Hard work, both physical and mental, is the name of the game. Because ultra running is so tough, most ultra runners keep a few tricks up their sleeves that they use during both training and competitions. Such tricks range from simple things like eating right and staying hydrated to specific workouts designed to improve performance on a particular ultra marathon course. Some runners train just to finish their first 100-mile race. Others, especially

those with more experience, focus on improving their best times at certain distances.

If you think you might want to run an ultra marathon someday, you can use the tips and tricks below to help you get started. Just remember, what works for one person may not work for the next. Experiment. See what works best for you.

Run, Run, and Run Some More

Question: What's the real secret to ultra running success?
Answer: Logging a lot of miles. It's true, the best way to win at this game is by going the distance. Get out there and run, walk, and hike as much as you can. See if you can find a few favorite routes and then mix it up a little. Run on the road one day and on the trail the next. Go for a long hike. And enjoy the scenery!

The Need for Speed

Most ultra marathoners don't consider speed a top priority. Still, the best ultra runners—those who win the competitions—often do what are called speed workouts. Speed workouts increase a runner's ability to go faster over longer distances, an important talent in a close race. Interestingly, speed workouts can also build strength. And strength—especially leg strength—is a handy thing to have whether you're trying to win a race or just trying to finish.

Repeats

There are many different kinds of speed workouts. One tried-and-true technique is to find a steep hill and run 50- to 75-meter

An ultra marathon runner trains by doing repeats up and down the steps of a stadium.

repeats on it once each week. Sprint up the hill (lifting your legs high) as fast as you can, then jog or walk slowly back to the bottom. As soon as you reach your starting point, turn around and do it all over again. Beginners might do three or four repeats in a row.

Experts—runners with really strong legs and lungs—can work their way up to ten or more repeats in a session, and they often run much farther than 75 meters! Some people prefer to run repeats on a flat track instead of on a hill. That way they can focus on speed without having to worry about rocks, roots, or the tricky footwork often required on trails.

Tempos

Another popular way to increase running speed and strength is through tempo training. Tempos, as they are called, typically consist of thirty minutes or so of continuous hard running sandwiched between a ten-minute warm-up and a ten-minute cooldown at jogging speed. They're done once or twice a week on hilly terrain. As a runner becomes stronger, he or she gradually increases running time. Eventually, racers who stick to their tempo workouts find that running fast for a long period of time becomes easy.

Perhaps the best way to get faster and stronger is the easiest of all. Enter a lot of races! Run short races, long races—it doesn't matter, just get out there and go!

Cross Training

Cross training is a technique that runners and other athletes use to keep their muscles balanced. Cross training helps prevent injuries that result from overworking one set of muscles while ignoring others. It also involves a rest day when you don't necessarily have to run, but you're still able to build strength and work toward your goal of completing an ultra marathon.

There are many different ways to cross train. You can work on upper-body areas like your arms, back, and shoulders through weight lifting, swimming, yoga, or stretching. You can practice speed walking, an important part of long-distance events, by hiking your favorite trails. You can build the big muscles in your legs (the quadriceps) by biking or skiing. Any kind of aerobic activity, in which you're moving a lot and using your lungs, is good for ultra marathon cross training.

Be mindful of your footing when running in the rain. Falling on slick and muddy paths can result in serious injury.

Other Running Tips

Running in the rain: Especially when running on a trail, beware of slick rocks, roots, and grass. Slow down on muddy or slippery sections to avoid wiping out.

Running uphill: Focus on something other than the pain. Think about a post-run feast or the view from the top of the hill. And pace yourself. If you feel yourself running out of steam, slow down or walk. During an ultra marathon race, always walk the uphill sections.

Running downhill: Put your arms out to your sides for balance on very steep downhills. You should look as though you're flying down the hill.

Running, day in and day out: Bring a motivated partner. Sometimes encouragement from a fellow runner is all it takes to make it through the miles.

Choosing an Ultra Marathon

Not every ultra marathon is a good first ultra. It pays to pick your first race carefully. First of all, don't start with the hardest ultra marathon you can find. Go easy on yourself. Choose a race that you can manage. Your goal is to finish, to cover 30, 40, 50, or 100 miles on foot. You don't need the extra challenge of a 10,000-foot vertical gain, river crossings, snow, or rain. Pick a race that's happening in the spring or fall, when the weather is nice and cool. Look for a race with a course that is relatively flat and that is well supported with aid stations and volunteers.

Building Up to the Big Day

Unless you are in great shape and have a lot of running experience, don't just go out and run an ultra marathon. Instead, work your way up to it by running shorter races first. Run a local 5K race. Then try a 10K. After that, give a half marathon a shot. When you're ready, do a marathon. Finally, with one or two marathons under your belt, go for the ultra.

And don't forget, rest days are just as important as your workouts and races. Take days off to let your body recover. If you don't, you may become injured.

Race-Day Strategies

Running the real thing on race day is just like training, only it is longer and harder. But don't worry. You'll have the support of all of your fellow ultra runners. If you cheer them on, they'll cheer you on.

As you race, try not to think about how far you have yet to run. If you do, it might become overwhelming and discouraging. Instead, try to break down the race into shorter parts. Focus on the next aid station. Set your sights on a tree up ahead and do what it takes to make your way past it. Each step counts. Take one step at a time and you'll eventually get to the finish.

In many ways, ultra marathon competitions aren't competitions at all. Most participants aren't there to try to win. They just want to challenge themselves while having a good time. Still, there are people who do treat every ultra marathon they enter as a race. These people are some of the best athletes in the world. They often cross the finish line hours ahead of the pack. Sometimes they're sponsored by major running-shoe companies or sports-drink manufacturers. Often they belong to an elite team of runners competing in major races throughout the world.

Above all, competitions are a great way to become involved in the ultra running scene. If you know you want to run in an ultra marathon race someday, it helps to have a specific event in

A runner, dressed as Elvis Presley, enjoys the applause he gets from the crowd as he finishes the Rock 'n' Roll Marathon on June 3, 2001.

mind. Without a race to look forward to, it can be difficult to stay focused on getting in shape and building the strength it takes to run long distances.

Race-Day Details

Race day (or days) at an ultra marathon is a festive event. For the most part, ultra racers are a different breed of runner. They're eccentric. They like to have fun while they run. It's not uncommon to find runners wearing strange costumes and singing songs as they go.

The night before the race is usually when the party begins. Many races include a pre-race banquet or dinner where runners eat as much lasagna, spaghetti, and other high-carbohydrate foods as they can fit on their plates. The runners try to get the inside scoop on the racecourse conditions and the weather forecast. They share game plans and strategies. Most of all, they get to know one another and make new friends.

Most races start early in the morning. Some races even begin in the middle of the night. When you're running 100 miles or more, it often doesn't matter when you start. You'll be running all day and all night anyway.

Most long races have checkpoints, or stations, through which racers must pass. The stations are a way for race organizers and volunteers to keep track of everyone on the course. Often there are cutoff times for each station. If you don't make it to the station before the cutoff time, you're automatically disqualified. Organizers set cutoff times mainly for safety reasons but also because they want to make sure the race is completed in a reasonable amount of time. Many races also provide runners with first aid, food, and drinks at checkpoints. Racers can stop in for a few minutes to refuel or, if they're injured and need help, they can get medical attention.

Where to Compete

Organized ultra marathon competitions are held every year all over the world. In fact, they're so common now that you should have no trouble finding a race near you. Most official ultra marathon events do not allow kids to race, but there's nothing

Most running associations hold races for children.

wrong with watching an ultra marathon and meeting the racers to learn what ultra marathon competitions are all about.

For a complete list of ultra-running competitions held throughout the world, go to the home page of UltraRunning Online (http://www.ultrarunning.com) and check out its calendar of events. Events are listed as early as one year before the race date. You can also stay aware of upcoming competitions by subscribing to *UltraRunning* magazine.

The All American Trail Running Association (www.trailrunner.com) also maintains a calendar of events for trail races of all lengths, long or short. Go to its Web site for details.

Finally, the American Ultrarunning Association (http://www.americanultra.org) has an ultra-running calendar on its home page. The calendar includes dates and links for national and world championship races as well as links to other Web pages listing ultra marathon competitions. For shorter running races just for kids, go to Kids Running Online (www.kidsrunning.com/krcalendar.html). The site includes a calendar of races, fun runs, and more.

Ultra Running to the Max: The Iditasport Extreme

The most remote, exposed, and—according to some—challenging ultra marathon in the world is right here in the United States: the Iditasport Extreme. Competitors in this famous Alaskan adventure race run 350 miles across the rugged Alaska Range. And they do it in true ultra style: in the middle of winter, towing an eighty-pound sled packed to the hilt with food, clothing, and survival gear. No motorized transportation is allowed; the entire course must be covered on foot.

The need for survival gear is clear when you consider what the racers face. For one, there's the cold. Below-zero temperatures are the norm. There's also the frigid arctic winds, the high probability of severe snowstorms, and the danger of falling into the many creeks and lakes that litter the vast tundra. Competitors get lost. They get injured. Many give up and drop out.

The secret to finishing the race, say past competitors, is in the mind. Conditioning is extremely important, of course, but often, when it comes right down to it, what separates those who cross the finish line from those who do not is mental strength.

If you think the Iditasport Extreme sounds cool, check out the event Web site (www.iditasport.com). There you'll find all kinds of information about the race, including details about how you can register to compete either on your own or as part of a team. And there's good news: Your entry fee—$1,000 for soloists, $5,000 for teams—includes a pre-race party, a T-shirt, meals at checkpoints along the course, a bed at the finish line, and, if necessary, an emergency evacuation. What a deal!

Portrait of an Ultra Runner: Peter's Story

I was very fat as a child. Although I was active, I did not exercise or take part in any sports. Then, at the age of eleven, I decided to change my life and lose weight. I began running. I started by running around the block and on local tracks. From then on, running was a part of my childhood and the sports I learned to play, including hockey, football, and track.

I entered my first ultra by accident. In 1995, I moved to Calgary, Alberta, Canada. Two days after arriving, I saw a sign for a 56-kilometer run called the Hot Ass 50. I registered on the day of the event. A guy on line at the registration table asked me what my longest run was, and I proudly stated, "About 1.5 hours!" After everyone stopped laughing, he told me to hang with him and I would finish. As the race began, I enjoyed myself and spent much time socializing at the water stations. But by the time we got to the turnaround, I felt really good and I went ahead of the pack. Two hours later, I was the first to cross the finish line. From that point on, I had the ultra bug.

Many runners claim that marathon running gives them a sense of peace and calm.

The toughest race I ever ran was last year in Hell, Michigan—the Dances with Dirt 80-kilometer trail run. It was a great race, but it was the only time in my life that I thought I was going to die. Whether it was because of the 100-degree temperature, my poor diet, not enough salt, or going out too fast, things went poorly. I remember praying at the top of one hill, and hanging on to a tree. But like always, I didn't quit and I proudly finished.

I became an ultra runner for many reasons. Running was an escape for me as a child—an escape from the poverty in which I lived and from the body I did not want. Today running lets me explore places that I otherwise would not see. I play in the local mountains and forests, even as an adult. Running has given me a better sense of who I am. By pushing myself beyond anything I thought would be physically possible, I've found an inner peace and calm. Running gives me the power to do anything I want!

Glossary

cross training Training for a specific sport by participating in other sports.

elevation Height above sea level.

endurance The ability to keep at something for a long time.

hydration Drinking to keep water in the body and replace fluids lost in exercise.

kilometer 1,000 meters or .62 miles.

marathon A race 26 miles, 385 yards in distance.

pace Speed.

rest day A day off.

switchback A sharp turn on a steep hill.

terrain Shape of the land.

trail running Running on trails.

training Practicing a sport to prepare for competition in that sport.

ultra Extreme, beyond the normal.

ultra marathon A running event longer than a marathon.

ultra running Running distances longer than a marathon.

All American Trail Running Association
P.O. Box 576
Crockett, CA 94525
(510) 787-1060
Web site: http://www.trailrunner.com

American Ultrarunning Association
USA Track & Field
One RCA Dome, Suite 140
Indianapolis, IN 46225
(317) 261-0500
Web site: http://www.americanultra.org

Association of Canadian Ultramarathoners
11 rue du Coteau
Hull, PQ J8Z 2V2
Canada
Web site: http://fox.nstn.ca/~dblaikie/uw-acu.html

Athletics Canada
Suite 606-1185 Eglinton Avenue East
Toronto, ON M3C 3C6
Canada
(416) 426-7181
Web site: http://www.canoe.ca/Athcan/home.html

Road Runners Club of America
510 North Washington Street
Alexandria, VA 22314
(703) 836-0558
Web site: http://www.rrca.org

Running USA
5522 Camino Cerralvo
Santa Barbara, CA 93111
(805) 964-0608
Web site: http://www.runningusa.org

Web Sites

Active.com
http://www.active.com/running

Canadian National 100K Running Team
http://www.100k.ca

Extreme Ultrarunning
http://www.extremeultrarunning.com

Hal Higdon.com
http://www.halhigdon.com

High School Runner
http://www.highschoolrunner.com

Kids Running
http://www.kidsrunning.com

New Runner
http://www.newrunner.com

Run 100s
http://www.run100s.com

Sky Runner
http://www.skyrunner.com

Ultramarathon World
http://fox.nstn.ca/~dblaikie

Ultra Runner
http://www.ultrarunner.net

The Ultrarunners Organization
http://www.ultrarunner.org

Camps for Kids

There are several nationwide athletic programs in the United States that sponsor general youth physical fitness and activity events, including running (although not ultra marathon running). They can be good places to start. Contact the programs listed below for more information.

Amateur Athletic Union
c/o Walt Disney World Resort
P.O. Box 10,000
Lake Buena Vista, FL 32830
(800) AAU-4USA (228-4872)
Web site: http://www.aausports.org

Hershey's Track & Field Youth Program
Hershey's Foods Corporation
175 Crystal A Drive
Hershey, PA 17033
(717) 534-8087
Web site: http://www.hersheys.com/trackandfield/home.shtml

The President's Challenge: Youth Physical Fitness Program
400 East 7th Street
Bloomington, IN 47405-3085
(800) 258-8146
Web site: http://www.indiana.edu/~preschal

USA Track & Field
1 RCA Dome, Suite 140
Indianapolis, IN 46225
(317) 261-0500
Web site: http://www.usatf.org/youth

Books

Boeder, Robert B. *Beyond the Marathon: The Grand Slam of Trail Ultrarunning.* Vienna, GA: Old Mountain Press, 1996.

Burfoot, Amby, ed. *Runner's World Complete Book of Running: Everything You Need to Know to Run for Fun, Fitness, and Competition.* Emmaus, PA: Rodale Press, 1997.

Glover, Bob, Jack Shepherd, and Shelly-Lynn Florence Glover. *The Runner's Handbook.* New York: Penguin USA, 1996.

Higdon, Hal. *Hal Higdon's How to Train: The Best Programs, Workouts, and Schedules for Runners of All Ages.* Emmaus, PA: Rodale Press, 1997.

Rodgers, Bill, and Scott Douglas. *Bill Rodgers' Lifetime Running Plan: Definite Programs for Runners of All Ages and Levels.* New York: HarperCollins, 1996.

Rodgers, Bill, and Scott Douglas. *The Complete Idiot's Guide to Jogging and Running.* New York: Alpha Books, 1998.

Magazines

Marathon & Beyond
411 Park Lane Drive
Champaign, IL 61820
(877) 972-4230
Web site: http://www.marathonandbeyond.com

Runner's World
135 North Sixth Street
Emmaus, PA 18098
(800) 666-2828
Web site: http://www.runnersworld.com

Trail Runner
North South Publications
5455 Spine Road, Mezzanine A
Boulder, CO 80301
(303) 499-8410
Web site: http://www.trailrunnermag.com

UltraRunning
P.O. Box 890238
Weymouth, MA 02189-0238
(888) 858-7203
Web site: http://www.ultrarunning.com

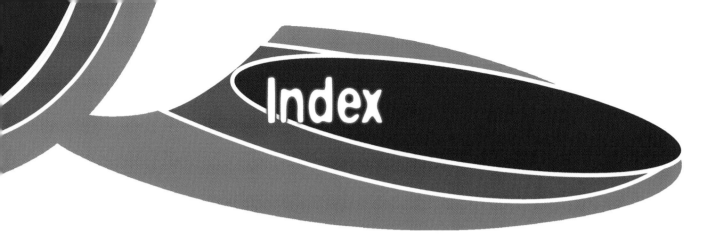

Index

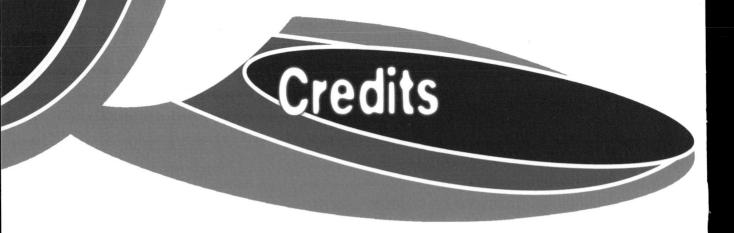

Credits

About the Author

Chris Hayhurst is a freelance writer living in Colorado.

Photo Credits

Cover, pp. 9, 46, 47 © AP/Wide World Photos; p. 2 © STL/Icon SMI; p. 5 © Lee Cohen/Allsport Photography; p. 6 © Simon Bruty/Allsport Photography; p. 8 © Neil Tingle/Action Plus/Icon SMI; p. 11 © Vince Streano/Corbis; pp. 15, 22, 24, 30, 39 by Maura Boruchow; pp. 14, 18 © David Klutho/SI/Icon SMI; pp. 20, 32 by Cindy Reiman; p. 25 © White/Phite/Int'l Stock; pp. 27, 37 © Corey Rich/Icon SMI; p. 29 © Miguelez/Icon SMI; p. 34 © G. Planchenault/Allsport Photography; p. 41 © Mike Powell/Allsport Photography; p. 43 © Jim Cummins/FPG by Getty Images; p. 49, 52 © Sport the Library/Icon SMI.

Design and Layout

Thomas Forget